Getting the Best

Your Air Fryer Oven

Toaster

50 Tasty and Healthy Recipes

to Cook Your Favorite Foods

without the Hassles of Frying

By

Linda Lavis

© **Copyright 2021 - All rights reserved.**

This document is geared towards providing exact and reliable information in regards to the topic and issue covered. The publication is sold with the idea that the publisher is not required to render accounting, officially permitted, or otherwise, qualified services. If advice is necessary, legal or professional, a practiced individual in the profession should be ordered.

—From a Declaration of Principles that was accepted and approved equally by a Committee of the American Bar Association and a Committee of Publishers and Associations.

In no way is it legal to reproduce, duplicate, or transmit any part of this document in either electronic means or in printed format. Recording of this publication is strictly prohibited, and any storage of this document is not allowed unless with written permission from the publisher. All rights reserved.

The information provided herein is stated to be truthful and consistent, in that any liability, in terms of inattention or otherwise, by any usage or abuse of any policies, processes, or directions contained within is the solitary and utter responsibility of the recipient reader. Under no circumstances will any legal responsibility or blame be held against the publisher for any reparation, damages, or monetary loss due to the information herein, either directly or indirectly.

Respective authors own all copyrights not held by the publisher.

The information herein is offered for informational purposes solely and is universal as so. The presentation of the information is without a contract or any type of guarantee assurance.

The trademarks that are used are without any consent, and the publication of the trademark is without permission or backing by the trademark owner. All trademarks and brands within this book are for clarifying purposes only and are owned by the owners themselves, not affiliated with this document.

Table of Contents

Introduction

Undoubtedly, an air fryer that consumes only a little bit of oil is an excellent option when it comes to reducing the amount of fat we usually consume in our food. In addition, its advantages also lie in the price, the utility and the benefits it provides, making it a good investment. It allows you to save money by not buying so much oil for cooking, cleaning and in the time you spend in the kitchen.

To get the most out of your air fryer, follow these tips:

- When cooking, don't overload the air fryer. Always use the factory recommendations.

- When placing the food in the basket, shake it before cooking. This way, the temperature will reach all the food evenly.

- Do not over roast food, as this can generate acrylamide, a toxic and possibly carcinogenic substance.

- Be careful. Avoid touching the air fryer when it is operating, as it is an appliance that requires a lot of heat to cook.

- Clean the air fryer after use, as this will prevent the accumulation of food debris and other debris that can generate bad odor and smoke.

- As a final tip, it is important that the foods are of similar size to avoid smaller foods cooking first or burning.

When preparing the recipes in this book, keep these tips in mind to improve your air fryer experience.

Chapter 1: Breakfast and

Brunch Recipes

1. Hidden-Egg Sandwich

(Ready in about 35 minutes | **Serving:** 2 | **Difficulty**:

Easy)

Per serving: **Kcal** 527, **Fat:** 25 g, **Net Carbs**: 56 g,

Protein: 22 g

Ingredients:

- 2 split bagels

- 2 teaspoon softened butter

- Cooking oil spray for a donut pan

- 2 eggs

- 2 teaspoon sriracha sauce

- 1 oz. cheese, divided and thinly sliced

- 1 pitted and smashed small avocado

- 1/3 cup sliced grape tomatoes

- ½ cup roughly chopped arugula

- Salt and pepper, as per taste

Instructions:

PREP AND COOK BAGELS:

1. Open bagels and take the interior bread out. Don't breakthrough. Spread the inside with butter and cook for around 3 minutes. Add siracha and top bagels with cheese.

BAKE EGGS:

2. Preheat the air fryer to 350°F. Use the cooking spray in a pan and break an egg inside a ramekin. Pour into pan and season with pepper and salt. Repeat with the rest of the eggs. Cook for around 11 minutes.

ASSEMBLY:

3. Mix sliced tomatoes, avocado, and arugula in a bowl. Season using pepper and salt. Add egg to each bagel half's bottom. Add the avocado mixture to the upper part of the bagels. Sandwich the bottoms and tops.

2. One Banana Bread

(Ready in about 35 minutes | **Serving:** 1 | **Difficulty:** Easy)

Per serving: Kcal 125, **Fat:** 4 g, **Net Carbs:** 20 g, **Protein:** 3 g

Ingredients:

- ¼ cup banana, mashed

- 1 egg

- 1 tablespoon Greek yogurt

- 1 tablespoon canola oil

- ¼ teaspoon vanilla extract, pure

- ½ cup whole-wheat white flour

- ¼ cup granulated white sugar

- ¼ teaspoon baking soda

- ¼ teaspoon ground cinnamon

- 1/8 teaspoon sea salt

Instructions:

1. Preheat the air fryer to 350°F and oil a loaf pan. Add all the ingredients to a bowl and stir to combine everything. Pour into the pan and cook for around 28 minutes.

3. Pita Peachy Pizzas

(Ready in about 13 minutes | **Serving:** 2 | **Difficulty**: Easy)

Per serving: **Kcal** 360, **Fat**: 11 g, **Net Carbs**: 56 g, **Protein**: 14 g

Ingredients:

- 4 whole-wheat mini pitas

- ½ teaspoon oil

- ¼ cup whole-milk ricotta cheese

- ¼ teaspoon lemon juice

- 1/16 teaspoon ground cinnamon

- 1 tablespoon raspberry preserves

- 2 large thinly sliced and pitted peaches

- 2 tablespoon fresh blueberries

- 1 tablespoon raw almonds, sliced

Instructions:

1. Preheat the air fryer to 400°F. Oil the mini pitas. Cook them for around 8 minutes. Mix cheese, cinnamon, and lemon juice in the meantime in a bowl. Spread raspberry preserves on pitas and add cheese mixture on top. Add peaches and top using blueberries. Sprinkle almonds on top.

4. Baked Eggs Marinara & Parmesan

(Ready in about 20 minutes | **Serving:** 4 | **Difficulty**: Easy)

Per serving: Kcal 284, **Fat**: 15 g, **Net Carbs**: 16 g, **Protein**: 19 g

Ingredients:

- 8 eggs

- 1 cup divided marinara sauce

- 1 tablespoon capers

- ¼ cup divided whipping cream

- ¼ cup divided parmesan cheese

- Salt

- Pepper

- Chives to taste

- Butter to grease

Instructions:

1. Spread four ramekins with butter. Add a quarter cup of marinara in each ramekin's base and top using capers. Break 2 eggs in each ramekin. Top with 1 tablespoon each of cheese and cream and sprinkle using pepper and salt. Cook for around 15 minutes at 400°F. Garnish using chives and enjoy with the cook.

5. Delicious Potatoes

(Ready in about 45 minutes | **Serving:** 4 | **Difficulty**:

Easy)

Per serving: **Kcal** 214, **Fat**: 6 g, **Net Carbs**: 15 g,

Protein: 4 g

Ingredients:

- 2 tablespoons olive oil

- 3 cubed potatoes

- 1 chopped yellow onion

- 1 red chopped bell pepper

- Salt and black pepper as per taste

- 1 teaspoon garlic powder

- 1 teaspoon sweet paprika

- 1 teaspoon onion powder

Instructions:

1. Oil the basket of the fryer lightly, and arrange potatoes. Season using pepper and salt. Add the rest of the ingredients and mix thoroughly. Cook for around 30 minutes at 370°F.

Chapter 2: Fish and

Seafood Recipes

6. Stuffed Calamari

(Ready in about 35 minutes | **Serving:** 4 | **Difficulty**:

Easy)

Per serving: Kcal: 322, **Fat:** 10 g, **Net Carbs:** 14 g,

Protein: 22 g

Ingredients:

- 4 big calamari, chopped, separated tentacles

  and tubes reserved

- 2 tablespoon parsley, chopped

- 5 oz. kale, chopped

- 2 minced garlic cloves

- 1 red chopped bell pepper

- 1 tablespoon olive oil

- 2 oz. tomato puree, canned

- 1 chopped yellow onion

- Salt

- Black pepper

Instructions:

1. Warm oil in a pan over moderate flame and cook garlic and onion for around 2 minutes. Add rest of ingredients except calamari tubes and cook for 10 more minutes. Stuff this mixture in calamari tubes and place it in a fryer. Broil for around 20 minutes at 360°F. Sprinkle with parsley and enjoy.

7. Mustard Salmon

(Ready in about 20 minutes | **Serving:** 1 | **Difficulty**:

Easy)

Per serving: Kcal: 300, **Fat:** 7 g, **Net Carbs**: 16 g,

Protein: 20 g

Ingredients:

- 1 big boneless salmon fillet

- Salt

- Black pepper

- 2 tablespoons mustard

- 1 tablespoon coconut oil

- 1 tablespoon maple extract

Instructions:

1. Season salmon using pepper and salt. Mix the rest of the ingredients in a bowl and brush over the salmon. Spray fish using cooking spray and place in a fryer. Broil for around 10 minutes at 370°F.

8. Crusted Salmon

(Ready in about 20 minutes | **Serving:** 4 | **Difficulty**: Easy)

Per serving: **Kcal:** 300, **Fat:** 17 g, **Net Carbs**: 20 g, **Protein**: 22 g

Ingredients:

- 1 cup chopped pistachios

- 4 salmon fillets

- ¼ cup lemon juice

- 2 tablespoon honey

- 1 teaspoon chopped dill

- Salt

- Black pepper

- 1 tablespoon mustard

Instructions:

1. Add all the ingredients to a bowl and toss to combine thoroughly. Transfer to a pan and place in a fryer. Broil for around 10 minutes at 350°F.

9. Salmon & Lemon Asparagus

(Ready in about 35 minutes | **Serving:** 4 | **Difficulty**:

Easy)

Per serving: **Kcal:** 314, **Fat**: 15 g, **Net Carbs**: 9 g,

Protein: 37 g

Ingredients:

- 1 lb. asparagus

- ½ teaspoon separated salt

- ½ teaspoon separated pepper

- 1 lemon

- 4 (8 oz. each) salmon fillets

Instructions:

1. Lay asparagus on the pan and sprinkle with half of pepper and salt. Dice lemon into slices of 1/4 inch and place on asparagus. Broil for around 10 minutes at 400°F. Sprinkle salmon with the rest of the pepper and salt. Add salmon on asparagus and broil for 20 additional minutes.

10. Cod & Pearl Onions

(Ready in about 25 minutes | **Serving:** 2 | **Difficulty**: Easy)

Per serving: Kcal: 270, **Fat:** 14 g, **Net Carbs**: 14 g, **Protein**: 22 g

Ingredients:

- 14 oz. pearl onions

- 2 medium cod fillets

- 1 tablespoon dried parsley

- 1 teaspoon thyme, dried

- Black pepper

- 8 oz. mushrooms, sliced

Instructions:

1. Add fish to a pan and add the rest of the ingredients. Toss to mix and coat the fish evenly. Place in the fryer and broil for around 15 minutes at 350°F.

Chapter 3: Snacks,

Appetizers, and Sides

11. Veggie Sticks with Yogurt

Herbed Dip

(Ready in about 30 minutes | **Serving**: 6 | **Difficulty**:

Easy)

Per serving: **Kcal:** 8, **Fat:** 9 g, **Net Carbs:** 1 g,

Protein: 1 g

Ingredients:

Yogurt Herbed Dip:

- 1 garlic clove

- 1 tablespoon mint leaves, fresh

- 7 oz. non-fat plain Greek yogurt

- 1 teaspoon lemon juice, fresh

- ¼ teaspoon kosher salt

Veggie Sticks:

- ½ cup unbleached all-purpose flour

- 3 well-beaten large eggs

- 1½ cups panko crumbs

- 2 tablespoon grated Pecorino Romano cheese

- 1 teaspoon dried oregano

- 1 teaspoon dried parsley

- ½ teaspoon kosher salt

- 1 zucchini medium, ¼" thick, and 3" long

- 10 trimmed beans string

- 1 avocado, in 8 slices

- A drizzle of olive oil

Instructions

1. Add mint and garlic to a blender and blend. Add lemon juice, salt, and yogurt and puree for around one minute. Transfer to a bowl and place in the fridge.

2. Place basket of fryer on a pan. Add eggs and flour to separate bowls. Mix panko, spices, salt, and cheese in another bowl. Dredge vegetables in flour, eggs, and then in a panko mixture. Transfer to pan and drizzle with oil. Cook for around 10 minutes at 375°F. Do it in two batches.

12. Cinnamon Walnuts

(Ready in about 25 minutes | **Serving**: 1 | **Difficulty**: Easy)

Per serving: **Kcal**: 199, **Fat**: 18.3 g, **Net Carbs**: 5.6 g, **Protein**: 6.8 g

Ingredients:

- 2 teaspoons maple syrup

- 1½ teaspoon olive oil

- ¼ teaspoon + 1/8 teaspoon powdered cinnamon

- 1/8 teaspoon sea salt

- 1 cup raw walnuts shelled

- ½ teaspoon granulated sugar organic

Instructions:

1. Preheat the fryer to 325°F. Coat a pan with oil. Mix everything except 1/8 teaspoon cinnamon and granulated sugar in a bowl. Pour mixture on a pan and cook for around 17 minutes. Combine cinnamon and sugar in the meantime. Sprinkle on nuts and enjoy.

13. Spiced Cashews

(Ready in about 20 minutes | **Serving**: 1 | **Difficulty**: Easy)

Per serving: Kcal: 175, **Fat:** 12.6 g, **Net Carbs**: 10.6 g, **Protein**: 5 g

Ingredients:

- Cooking spray

- 2 teaspoons maple syrup pure

- ½ teaspoon EVOO

- 1 teaspoon yellow curry powder

- ¼ teaspoon cumin

- ¼ teaspoon ground ginger

- ¼ teaspoon sea salt

- 1 cup unsalted raw cashews

Instructions:

1. Preheat the fryer to 325°F. Spray a pan with oil. Mix all the ingredients in a bowl, adding cashews at last, and mix. Pour mixture on the pan and cook for around 15 minutes. Cool them before storing or eating.

14. Chex Mix

(Ready in about 90 minutes | **Serving**: 5 | **Difficulty**: Hard)

Per serving: Kcal: 140, **Fat:** 7.4 g, **Net Carbs**: 16.6 g, **Protein**: 3.1 g

Ingredients:

- 1 cup Chex® cereal corn

- 1 cup Chex® cereal rice

- 1 cup Chex® cereal wheat

- ½ cup mixed nuts

- ½ cup pretzels mini

- ½ cup bagel chips

- 2 tablespoons melted butter

- 2 teaspoons Worcestershire sauce

- ½-¾ teaspoon season salt

- ¼ teaspoon garlic powder

- 1/8-¼ teaspoon onion powder

Instructions:

1. Preheat the fryer to 250°F. Combine nuts, cereals, bagel chips, and pretzels in a bowl. Microwave butter for around 20 seconds in a separate bowl and add the rest of the ingredients to it. Pour this mixture over cereal and mix. Pour mixture into the pan and cook for around 1 hour.

15. Seasoned Tortilla Chips

(Ready in about 12 minutes | **Serving**: 1 | **Difficulty**:

Easy)

Per serving: **Kcal**: 150, **Fat**: 6.1 g, **Net Carbs**: 20 g,

Protein: 3 g

Ingredients:

- 1 tortilla

- Oil

- Any seasoning mix

- Sea salt

Instructions:

1. Preheat the fryer to 350°F. Brush tortilla with oil and add seasoning. Cut them into triangles. Arrange in the basket of the fryer in such a way that they do not overlap. Cook for around 8 minutes. They will turn slightly brown. Allow them to cool in the pan before eating.

16. Potato Spread

(Ready in about 20 minutes | **Serving**: 10 |

Difficulty: Easy)

Per serving: **Kcal**: 200, **Fat**: 3 g, **Net Carbs**: 20 g,

Protein: 11 g

Ingredients:

- 19 oz. drained garbanzo beans, canned

- 1 cup peeled sweet potatoes, chopped

- ¼ cup of tahini

- 2 tablespoon lemon juice

- 1 tablespoon olive oil

- 5 minced garlic cloves

- ½ teaspoon ground cumin

- 2 tablespoon water

- Salt

- White pepper

Instructions:

1. Add potatoes to the basket of the fryer and cook them for around 15 minutes at 360°F. Add to food processor and pulse. Add the rest of the ingredients and pulse thoroughly.

17. Loaded Fries

(Ready in about 30 minutes | **Serving**: 2 | **Difficulty**:

Easy)

Per serving: **Kcal:** 229, **Fat**: 11.5 g, **Net Carbs**: 26

g, **Protein**: 6.9 g

Ingredients:

Seasoned Fries:

- 8 oz. crinkle cut frozen fries

- 2 teaspoon vegetable oil

- ¼ teaspoon each cumin, dried oregano, sea salt,

  garlic powder, black pepper

Yogurt Sauce:

- ¼ cup Greek yogurt, plain

- 2 teaspoons lemon juice

- 1/8 teaspoon garlic powder

- 1 tablespoon chopped parsley, fresh

- Salt

- Pepper

Toppings:

- ¼ cup feta, crumbled

- 1 finely chopped shallot

- ¼ cup cucumber, chopped

- ¼ cup bell pepper, chopped

- 2 tablespoon Kalamata olives, sliced

- Chopped fresh parsley to taste

- Lemon wedges

Instructions:

1. Combine seasoning, oil, and fries in a bowl and stir. Arrange fries in a pan in one layer and cook for around 15 minutes at 350°F. Mix the rest of the ingredients in a bowl to make the sauce. Place half fries with half sauce and add another layer of fries and sauce.

18. Parmesan Crisps

(Ready in about 13 minutes | **Serving**: 6 | **Difficulty**: Easy)

Per serving: Kcal: 125, **Fat**: 8.2 g, **Net Carbs**: 1 g, **Protein**: 11.4 g

Ingredients:

- 6 tablespoon parmesan cheese shredded

Instructions:

1. Preheat the fryer to 350°F. Add cheese to a pan and cook for around 5 minutes. Take out of the oven and cool before storing or eating.

19. Rosemary Cashews

(Ready in about 26 minutes | **Serving**: 1 | **Difficulty**: Easy)

Per serving: **Kcal:** 183, **Fat:** 13 g, **Net Carbs**: 11.4 g, **Protein**: 5.4 g

Ingredients:

- 1 cup unsalted raw cashews

- 1 tablespoon fresh rosemary, finely chopped

- 2 teaspoon maple syrup, pure

- 1/8 teaspoon red pepper, crushed

- ¼ teaspoon sea salt

- Cooking spray

Instructions:

1. Preheat the fryer to 325°F. Spray a pan with oil
   and combine all the ingredients in a bowl. Mix
   to coat everything. Pour mixture over the pan
   and cook for around 18 minutes. They will turn
   dark but remain shiny. Allow them to cool
   before storing or eating.

20. Roasted Chickpeas

(Ready in about 50 minutes | **Serving**: 4 | **Difficulty**:

Moderate)

Per serving: Kcal: 120, **Fat:** 2.6 g, **Net Carbs**: 19.3

g, **Protein**: 5.3 g

Ingredients:

- 15 oz. reduced-sodium canned chickpeas, rinsed

- 1 ½ teaspoon grapeseed oil

- 1 ½ teaspoon any seasoning

Instructions:

1. Preheat the fryer to 375°F. Spread chickpeas on

    the kitchen towel and pat dry. Arrange in a layer

    in a pan. Cook chickpeas for around 30 minutes.

    Shake the pan after every 10 minutes. They will

    turn soft. Transfer them to a bowl and add

    seasoning blend. Mix to coat and add back to the

    pan. Cook for five more minutes.

21. Nachos

(Ready in about 20 minutes | **Serving**: 1 | **Difficulty**:

Easy)

Per serving: **Kcal:** 148, **Fat**: 8.8 g, **Net Carbs**: 11 g,

Protein: 6.7 g

Ingredients:

- 1 6" corn tortilla

- Oil to grease

- Sea salt

- 3 tablespoon shredded cheese

Optional Toppings:

- Jalapeño slices

- Chopped tomatoes

- Salsa

- Guacamole

- Sour cream

Instructions

1. Bake the chips.

2. Preheat the fryer to 350°F. Oil a pan gently and brush tortillas with oil. Season with salt and slice into triangles. Arrange them in a single layer in the pan. Cook for around 8 minutes and flip and cook for 4 additional minutes. Take the pan out and let them cool. Sprinkle chips with cheese and cook for 2 more minutes.

Chapter 4: Beef Recipes

22. Steaks and Cabbage

(Ready in about 20 minutes | **Serving**: 4 | **Difficulty**:

Easy)

Per serving: **Kcal**: 282, **Fat**: 6 g, **Net Carbs**: 14 g,

Protein: 6 g

Ingredients:

- ½ lb. sirloin steak, strips

- 2 teaspoons cornstarch

- 1 tablespoon peanut oil

- 2 cups chopped green cabbage

- 1 yellow chopped bell pepper

- 2 chopped green onions

- 2 minced garlic cloves

- Salt

- Black pepper

Instructions:

1. Mix pepper, salt, cabbage, and peanut oil in a bowl. Add to the basket in the air fryer and broil for around 4 minutes at 370°F. Transfer mixture to a bowl. Add the rest of the ingredients with steak and broil for around 5 minutes. Take out on a plate and top with cabbage mixture.

23. Short Ribs with Beer Sauce

(Ready in about 60 minutes | **Serving**: 6 | **Difficulty**: Moderate)

Per serving: **Kcal**: 300, **Fat**: 7 g, **Net Carbs**: 18 g, **Protein**: 23 g

Ingredients:

- 4 lbs. diced into pieces short ribs

- 1 chopped yellow onion

- Black pepper and salt

- 1/4 cup tomato paste

- 1 cup dark beer

- 1 cup chicken stock

- 1 bay leaf

- 6 chopped thyme springs

- 1 dried Portobello mushroom

Instructions:

1. Warm a pan over moderate flame and add onion, tomato paste, stock, mushroom, beer, thyme, and bay leaves. Simmer and add ribs. Place in the fryer and broil for around 40 minutes at 350°F.

24. Beef Stew

(Ready in about 30 minutes | **Serving**: 4 | **Difficulty**: Easy)

Per serving: Kcal: 260, **Fat**: 5 g, **Net Carbs**: 20 g, **Protein**: 22 g

Ingredients:

- 2 lbs. beef meat, medium chunks

- 2 chopped carrots

- 4 chopped potatoes

- Salt

- Black pepper

- ¼ veggie stock

- ½ teaspoon smoked paprika

- A handful chopped thyme

Instructions:

1. Mix all the ingredients in a dish and add to the basket of the air fryer. Broil for around 20 minutes at 375°F.

25. Meatballs Sandwich

(Ready in about 32 minutes | **Serving**: 4 | **Difficulty**:

Easy)

Per serving: **Kcal:** 380, **Fat:** 5 g, **Net Carbs**: 34 g,

Protein: 20 g

Ingredients:

- 3 sliced baguettes, halfway through

- 14 oz. minced beef

- 7 oz. tomato sauce

- 1 chopped small onion

- 1 whisked egg

- 1 tablespoon breadcrumbs

- 2 tablespoon grated cheddar cheese

- 1 tablespoon oregano, chopped

- 1 tablespoon olive oil

- Salt

- Black pepper

- 1 teaspoon thyme, dried

- 1 teaspoon basil, dried

Instructions:

1. Mix everything except tomato sauce and oil in a bowl and make meatballs. Oil the basket and place meatballs in the basket. Broil them for around 12 minutes at 375°F. Pour the tomato sauce and broil for 10 more minutes. Spread them on baguettes and eat.

Chapter 5: Bakery and

Desserts

26. Cranberry Cookies

(Ready in about 30 minutes | **Serving:** 12 | **Difficulty**: Easy)

Per serving: Kcal: 42, **Fat:** 2 g, **Net Carbs**: 7 g, **Protein**: 1 g

Ingredients:

- 1 + ½ tablespoon softened unsalted butter

- ¼ cup packed brown sugar

- ½ teaspoon orange zest

- 2 tablespoons orange juice, freshly squeezed

- ¼ teaspoon vanilla extract

- Egg white

- ¼ cup whole-wheat white flour

- ¾ cup quick oats

- ½ teaspoon cinnamon

- ¼ teaspoon table salt

- ¼ teaspoon baking soda

- 2 tablespoons roughly chopped dried cranberries

Instructions:

1. Mix all the ingredients in a bowl. Preheat the fryer at 350°F and oil the pan. Pour the mixture into the pan and bake the cookies for 12 to 15 minutes until light brown. Cool and serve.

27. Apple Crisp

(Ready in about 40 minutes | **Serving:** 1 | **Difficulty:**
Easy)

Per serving: Kcal: 313, **Fat:** 12 g, **Net Carbs:** 54 g,
Protein: 2 g

Ingredients:

- Cooking spray

- 1 medium sliced apple

- 1 tablespoon white flour

- 1 tablespoon brown sugar

- 1 teaspoon ground cinnamon

- A pinch of salt

- 2 tablespoons water

- 1 tablespoon butter

- 1 tablespoon ice cream caramel topping

Instructions:

1. Preheat the fryer at 375°F and use cooking spray to oil the pan. Align apple slices in the pan. Mix all the ingredients in a bowl and spread over apples. Sprinkle water over it and bake the apples for 30 minutes. Serve with caramel sauce.

28. Baked Apples

(Ready in about 40 minutes | **Serving:** 4 | **Difficulty**: Easy)

Per serving: Kcal: 243, **Fat:** 9 g, **Net Carbs**: 42 g, **Protein**: 3 g

Ingredients:

- 4 firm sweet-tart apples

- ¼ cup rolled oats

- 2 tablespoons chopped pecans

- 1 tablespoon all-purpose unbleached flour

- 1 tablespoon brown sugar

- 2 pinches of powdered cinnamon

- A pinch of kosher salt

- A pinch of ground nutmeg

- 2 tablespoons cubed unsalted butter

Instructions:

1. Cover the baking pan with parchment paper. Core the apples. Mix all the ingredients together and fill the apples with this mixture. Pour the apples into the pan and bake for 35 minutes at 350°F until crispy and brown.

29. Fresh Blueberry Muffins

(Ready in about 30 minutes | **Serving:** 6 | **Difficulty**: Easy)

Per serving: **Kcal:** 269, **Fat**: 10 g, **Net Carbs**: 17 g, **Protein**: 15 g

Ingredients:

- 1 cup + 1 tablespoon all-purpose unbleached flour, divided

- 1½ teaspoon baking powder

- ¼ teaspoon kosher salt

- A pinch of powder cinnamon

- 4 tablespoons unsalted butter

- ¾ cup sugar granulates

- 1 egg

- ½ teaspoon vanilla extract pure

- ¼ cup of whole milk

- 1 cup fresh blueberries

- Softened butter

Instructions:

1. First, mix 1 cup of the flour, baking powder, salt, and cinnamon. Then mix the rest of the ingredients in a separate bowl and combine these two mixtures. Oil the muffin tins, fill them with the mixture, and bake for 25 minutes at 325°F until golden. Cool and serve.

30. Cinnamon Bites

(Ready in about 1 hour 15 minutes | **Serving:** 16 | **Difficulty**: Hard)

Per serving: **Kcal:** 66, **Fat**: 3 g, **Net Carbs:** 8 g, **Protein**: 1 g

Ingredients:

- ¾ teaspoon dry yeast active

- ½ +1½ teaspoon sugar granulates

- 1 tablespoon whole milk warm

- ¾ cup bread flour

- 2 pinches of kosher salt

- 2 pinches of powdered cinnamon

- pinch powdered nutmeg

- 1 lightly beaten large egg

- 2 tablespoons buttermilk

- ½ teaspoon vanilla extract pure

- 1 tablespoon unsalted cubed butter

- Non-stick spray

- 2 tablespoons melted butter

- Cinnamon sugar

Instructions:

1. Mix yeast, sugar, and milk and leave it for 5 to 10 minutes. Mix flour, the remaining sugar, salt, cinnamon, and nutmeg in another bowl. Mix these mixtures and add the rest of the ingredients. Knead the mixture to form the dough. Put this dough in a bowl and rest for 1 hour after covering it with plastic wrap. Oil the baking sheet. Roll small pieces of dough with your hand and cover them with a plastic sheet again. Bake them in a fryer and brush them with butter and cinnamon sugar. Serve.

31. Ginger Scones

(Ready in about 40 minutes | **Serving:** 8 | **Difficulty**:

Easy)

Per serving: **Kcal:** 304, **Fat:** 9 g, **Net Carbs**: 48 g,

Protein: 5 g

Ingredients:

- ½ cups, all-purpose unbleached flour

- ¼ cup sugar granulates

- 2 teaspoons baking powder

- ¼ teaspoon kosher salt

- 2 tablespoons ginger finely chopped

- 6 tablespoons cubed unsalted butter, cold

- 2/3 cup buttermilk

- 1 lightly beaten large egg

- 1 cup cherries dried

- 1 beaten egg white

Instructions:

1. Prepare the pan with parchment paper. Pulse flour, sugar, baking powder, salt, ginger, and butter for 10 seconds. Add buttermilk and egg into the mixture and pulse again. Pour this dough into a tray and divide it into 8 equal pieces. Brush egg white on them. Bake for 30 minutes at 350°F in the pan until golden brown.

32. Chocolate Cake

(Ready in about 30 minutes | **Serving:** 12 | **Difficulty**: Easy)

Per serving: **Kcal:** 399, **Fat:** 25 g, **Net Carbs**: 41 g, **Protein**: 3 g

Ingredients:

Chocolate Cake:

- 1 cup all-purpose unbleached flour

- 1/3 cup sifted cocoa powder

- 1 teaspoon espresso powder

- ½ teaspoon baking soda

- ¼ teaspoon baking powder

- ¼ teaspoon kosher salt

- 8 tablespoons cubed unsalted butter

- ½ cup granulated sugar

- ¼ cup light brown packed sugar

- 1 egg

- 1 egg yolk

- 1 teaspoon vanilla extract, pure

- ½ cup buttermilk

Frosting:

- 16 tablespoons + 2 tablespoons cubed unsalted

  butter

- 1½ cups sifted confectioners' sugar

- ¼ teaspoon kosher salt

- ½ teaspoon vanilla extract pure

- 4 tablespoons heavy cream

- ¼ cup granulated sugar

- Water

- Sea salt

Instructions:

1. Cover the cake pan with oil. Mix flour, cocoa powder, espresso powder, baking soda, baking powder, and salt in a bowl. Whisk butter and sugar with a mixer until creamy. Keep on adding the rest of the ingredients in this batter while continuously mixing. Pour this in the pan and bake for 20 minutes at 350°F. Put this in the refrigerator. For the frosting, mix butter, sugar, salt, vanilla extract, and cream until fluffy. Make sugar syrup by adding granulated sugar into

water and heating it. Mix this syrup, butter, and cream, and cool this. Add this mixture to the frosting. Cut the cake into two halves and put frosting between the two layers, and cover the whole cake with frosting. Sprinkle caramel sauce and sea salt on it and serve.

Chapter 6: Pork and Lamb

Recipes

33. Pork Burgers

(Ready in about 55 minutes | **Serving:** 4 | **Difficulty**:

Moderate)

Per serving: Kcal: 325, **Fat:** 12 g, **Net Carbs:** 13.7

g, **Protein**: 24.3 g

Ingredients:

- 300 g mince mixed (beef and pork)

- Small diced onion

- 1 teaspoon garlic puree

- 1 teaspoon tomato puree

- 1 teaspoon mustard

- 1 teaspoon basil

- 1 teaspoon mixed herbs

- Pepper and salt

- 25 g cheddar cheese

- 4 bread buns

- Salad (for topping)

Instructions:

1. Add seasonings and mince mixed in a bowl and mix. Make four burgers out of the mixture and place in a pan. Place in fryer and toast for around 25 minutes at 340°F. Reduce temperature to 300°F and toast for 20 more minutes. Add cheese, salad, and bun.

34. Provencal Pork

(Ready in about 25 minutes | **Serving:** 2 | **Difficulty**:

Easy)

Per serving: **Kcal:** 300, **Fat:** 8 g, **Net Carbs**: 21 g,

Protein: 23 g

Ingredients:

- 1 sliced red onion

- 1 diced into strips yellow bell pepper

- 1 diced into strips green bell pepper

- Black pepper and salt

- 2 teaspoons Provencal herbs

- 1/2 tablespoon mustard

- 1 tablespoon olive oil

- 7 oz. pork tenderloin

Instructions:

1. Add yellow and green pepper, onion, and salt to a pan. Add half amount of oil and Provencal herbs. Mix everything. Season pork using pepper, salt, remaining oil, and mustard. Mix and add to vegetables. Place in fryer and toast for around 15 minutes at 370°F.

35. Lamb Chops

(Ready in about 20 minutes | **Serving:** 4 | **Difficulty**: Easy)

Per serving: Kcal: 231, **Fat:** 7 g, **Net Carbs**: 14 g, **Protein**: 23 g

Ingredients:

- 3 tablespoon olive oil

- 8 lamb chops

- Black pepper and salt

- 4 minced garlic cloves

- 1 tablespoon chopped oregano

- 1 tablespoon chopped coriander

Instructions:

1. Add all the ingredients in a bowl with lamb and toss to coat the lamb. Transfer lamb to basket of fryer and toast for around 10 minutes at 400°F.

36. Lamb with Brussels Sprouts

(Ready in about 1 hour 10 minutes | **Serving:** 4 |

Difficulty: Hard)

Per serving: Kcal: 440, **Fat**: 23 g, **Net Carbs**: 2 g,

Protein: 49 g

Ingredients:

- 2 lbs. scored leg of lamb

- 2 tablespoons olive oil

- 1 tablespoon chopped rosemary

- 1 tablespoon chopped lemon thyme

- 1 minced garlic clove

- 1 1/2 lb. trimmed Brussels sprouts

- 1 tablespoon melted butter

- 1/2 cup sour cream

- Black pepper and salt

Instructions:

1. Season lamb with seasonings and brush oil over them. Place in basket of fryer and toast for around 1 hour at 300°F. Place in plate aside and add Brussels sprouts with rest of ingredients in a pan and toast for around 10 minutes at 400°F. Enjoy sprouts on the side with lamb.

Chapter 7: Poultry Recipes

37. Fresh Mix

(Ready in about 32 minutes | **Serving:** 4 | **Difficulty**:

Easy)

Per serving: **Kcal:** 172, **Fat:** 4 g, **Net Carbs**: 12 g,

Protein: 4 g

Ingredients:

- 2 boneless, skinless, and cubed chicken breasts

- 8 sliced button mushrooms

- 1 chopped bell pepper

- 1 tablespoon olive oil

- ½ teaspoon dried thyme

- 10 oz. alfredo sauce

- 6 slices bread

- 2 tablespoons soft butter

Instructions:

1. In your fryer, mix chicken with mushrooms, bell pepper and oil, toss to coat well and air fry at 350°F for 15 minutes. Transfer chicken mixture to a bowl, add thyme and alfredo sauce, toss, return to air fryer and cook at 350°F for 4 minutes more. Spread butter on bread slices, add it to the fryer, butter side up and air fry for four minutes. Arrange toasted bread slices on a platter, top each with chicken mixture and serve. Enjoy!

38. Buttermilk Chicken

(Ready in about 28 minutes | **Serving:** 4 | **Difficulty**:

Easy)

Per serving: **Kcal:** 200, **Fat**: 3 g, **Net Carbs**: 14 g,

Protein: 4 g

Ingredients:

- 1½ lb. chicken thighs

- 2 cups buttermilk

- Salt

- Black pepper

- cayenne pepper pinch

- 2 cups refined flour

- 1 tablespoon baking powder

- 1 tablespoon sweet paprika

- 1 tablespoon garlic powder

Instructions:

1. In a bowl, add chicken thighs, buttermilk, salt, pepper, and cayenne, toss and leave for six hours. In another bowl, mix flour, paprika, baking powder, garlic powder and stir. Coat chicken in the flour mix, arrange them in your fryer and toast at 360°F for eight minutes. Turn it and cook them for further 10 minutes.

39. Chicken Pie

(Ready in about 26 minutes | **Serving:** 4 | **Difficulty**: Easy)

Per serving: **Kcal:** 300, **Fat**: 5 g, **Net Carbs**: 14 g, **Protein**: 7 g

Ingredients:

- 2 skinless, boneless chicken thighs and cubed

- 1 chopped carrot

- 1 chopped yellow onion

- 2 chopped potatoes

- 2 chopped mushrooms

- 1 teaspoon soy sauce

- Salt

- Black pepper

- 1 teaspoon Italian seasoning

- ½ teaspoon garlic powder

- 1 teaspoon Worcestershire sauce

- 1 tablespoon flour

- 1 tablespoon milk

- 2 sheets puff pastry

- 1 tablespoon melted butter

Instructions:

1. Heat a pan, add potatoes, carrots, and onion, and cook for two minutes. Add chicken and mushrooms, salt, soy sauce, pepper, Italian seasoning, garlic powder, Worcestershire sauce, flour, and milk. Mix well put it aside. Put one

puff pastry sheet on the bottom of the fryer's pan and trim excess. Put the chicken mix on top of other puff pastry sheets. Put in the fryer and cook at 360°F for six minutes.

40. Lunch Fajitas

(Ready in about 20 minutes | **Serving:** 4 | **Difficulty**: Easy)

Per serving: **Kcal:** 317, **Fat**: 6 g, **Net Carbs**: 14 g, **Protein**: 4 g

Ingredients:

- 1 teaspoon garlic powder

- ¼ teaspoon cumin, ground

- ½ teaspoon chili powder

- Salt

- Black pepper

- ¼ teaspoon coriander, ground

- 1 lb. chicken breasts, strips

- 1 red sliced bell pepper

- 1 green sliced bell pepper

- 1 chopped yellow onion

- 1 tablespoon lime juice

- Cooking spray

- 4 warmed up tortillas

- Salsa

- Sour cream

- 1 cup torn lettuce leaves

Instructions:

1. Take chicken, garlic powder, cumin, chili, salt, pepper, coriander, lime juice, red bell pepper, green bell pepper and onion, toss and leave aside for ten minutes. Transfer it to the fryer and spray cooking spray. Mix and toast at 400°F for around 10 minutes. Place tortillas and split chicken mix, salsa, sour cream, and lettuce. Wrap it and serve.

41. Chicken Salad

(Ready in about 30 minutes | **Serving:** 4 | **Difficulty**: Easy)

Per serving: **Kcal:** 372, **Fat**: 6 g, **Net Carbs**: 17 g, **Protein**: 6 g

Ingredients:

- 2 hulled corn ears

- 1 lb. boneless chicken tenders

- Olive oil

- Salt

- Black pepper

- 1 teaspoon sweet paprika

- 1 tablespoon brown sugar

- ½ teaspoon garlic powder

- ½ head iceberg lettuce, medium strips

- ½ head romaine lettuce, medium strips

- 1 cup drained black beans, canned

- 1 cup shredded cheddar cheese

- 3 tablespoons chopped cilantro

- 4 chopped green onions

- 12 sliced cherry tomatoes

- ¼ cup ranch dressing

- 3 tablespoons BBQ sauce

Instructions:

1. Place corn in the fryer, put oil, toss, toast at 400°F for around 10 minutes. Put the chicken in the fryer's basket, add salt, pepper, brown sugar, paprika and garlic powder, toss, sprinkle oil and toast at 400°F for ten minutes and chop them. Put corn in a bowl, add chicken, iceberg lettuce, romaine lettuce, black beans, cheese, cilantro, tomatoes, onions, BBQ sauce and ranch dressing, then mix well and serve.

42. Philadelphia Chicken

(Ready in about 40 minutes | **Serving:** 4 | **Difficulty**:

Easy)

Per serving: **Kcal:** 300, **Fat:** 8 g, **Net Carbs**: 20 g,

Protein: 6 g

Ingredients:

- 1 teaspoon olive oil

- 1 sliced yellow onion

- 2 boneless, skinless chicken breasts, sliced

- Salt

- Black pepper

- 1 tablespoon Worcestershire sauce

- 14 oz. pizza dough

- 1½ cups grated cheddar cheese

- ½ cup cheese sauce, jarred

Instructions:

1. Preheat fryer at 400°F, add half of the oil and onions and toast for around 8 minutes. Put chicken pieces, Worcestershire sauce, salt, and pepper, mix and cook for 8 minutes more. Make pizza dough in a rectangle. Spread the cheese, chicken, onion, and sauce over the dough. Make the shape of the dough. Put the roll in the fryer's basket, brush it with oil and toast at 370°F for around 12 minutes.

Chapter 8: Vegetable

Recipes

43. Baked Asparagus

(Ready in about 25 minutes | **Serving:** 4 | **Difficulty**:

Easy)

Per serving: **Kcal:** 77, **Fat**: 6 g, **Net Carbs**: 5 g,

Protein: 3 g

Ingredients:

- 1 lb. trimmed fresh asparagus

- Cooking spray

- Salt

- Pepper

- 2 tablespoons butter

- 1 tablespoon soy sauce

- 1 teaspoon balsamic vinegar

Instructions:

1. Preheat the fryer to 400°F. Set all the asparagus on a baking sheet, then oil them using cooking spray. Toast the asparagus for around 12 minutes in the preheated fryer. Melt the butter in a pan over a low flame, then remove the heat and stir in balsamic vinegar soy. Put over your toasted asparagus to serve.

44. Portobello Burgers

(Ready in about 50 minutes | **Serving:** 4 | **Difficulty:** Moderate)

Per serving: Kcal: 490, **Fat:** 33 g, **Net Carbs**: 39 g, **Protein**: 14 g

Ingredients:

- 2 beets medium

- ¼ cup olive oil

- 2 tablespoons balsamic vinegar

- 1 teaspoon dried rosemary

- 2 minced garlic cloves

- 4 Portobello mushroom caps

- ½ cup goat cheese

- 4 toasted split sandwich buns

- 1 ½ cups spinach leaves

- 3 tablespoons mayonnaise

- 2 minced garlic cloves

- 2 juiced limes

Instructions:

1. Preheat an air fryer to 400°F. Remove the tops of the beets and put them in a baking dish with sufficient water. Toast the beets in the preheated fryer for around 40 to 50 minutes. Preheat the fryer's basket again. Mixed the rosemary balsamic vinegar, 2 minced garlic cloves, and olive oil together in a bowl. Pour about half of the mixture over mushroom caps. Toast mushrooms for around 7 minutes. Roll the mushrooms mixture over the tops of the caps. Return to the fryer and toast for around 5 minutes more. Pour cheese on sandwich rolls. Roll every sandwich with a portion of the sliced beets and the spinach. Stir the lime juice, mayonnaise, and garlic together in a bowl. Take

the two halves together to form your sandwiches to serve.

45. Balsamic Bruschetta

(Ready in about 15 minutes | **Serving**: 8 | **Difficulty**: Easy)

Per serving: **Kcal**: 194, **Fat**: 3 g, **Net Carbs**: 35 g, **Protein**: 8 g

Ingredients:

- 8 diced plum tomatoes

- 1/3 cup fresh basil, chopped

- ¼ cup Parmesan cheese, shredded

- 2 minced garlic cloves

- 1 tablespoon balsamic vinegar

- 1 teaspoon olive oil

- ¼ teaspoon kosher salt

- ¼ teaspoon black pepper, freshly ground

- 1 sliced and a toasted loaf of French bread

Instructions:

1. Mix together the garlic, Parmesan cheese, tomatoes, and basil in a bowl. Add the pepper, olive oil, balsamic vinegar, kosher salt, and mix. Serve on toasted slices of bread.

46. Vegetarian Sandwich

(Ready in about 25 minutes | **Serving:** 6 | **Difficulty**: Easy)

Per serving: **Kcal:** 222, **Fat:** 9 g, **Net Carbs**: 24 g, **Protein**: 13 g

Ingredients:

- 6 sourdough bread slices, toasted

- 3 tablespoons pesto sauce

- 1 small sliced eggplant

- 1 small sliced bell pepper

- 1 medium sliced red onion

- 2 sliced tomatoes

- 1 cup fresh mushrooms, sliced

- 6 mozzarella cheese slices

- 4 garlic cloves

- Dried oregano

- Dried basil

- Salt

- Pepper

Instructions:

1. Preheat the fryer to 340°F. Pour every bread slice with the pesto sauce and arrange the slices on a baking sheet. Coat every slice with red bell pepper, eggplant, tomatoes, mushrooms, red onion, and cheese. Chop the garlic on top of the cheese, and season with, salt, basil, pepper, and

oregano. Broil for around 5 minutes in the preheated fryer.

47. California Melt

(Ready in about 17 minutes | **Serving:** 4 | **Difficulty**: Easy)

Per serving: **Kcal:** 335, **Fat:** 23 g, **Net Carbs**: 21 g, **Protein**: 16 g

Ingredients:

- 4 lightly toasted whole-grain bread slices

- 1 sliced avocado

- 1 cup mushrooms, sliced

- 1/3 cup toasted almonds, sliced

- 1 sliced tomato

- 4 Swiss cheese slices

Instructions:

1. Preheat the fryer to 320°F. Put the toasted bread out, then roll every slice of bread with one-fourth of the mushrooms, avocado, tomato slices, and almonds. Also, add cheese on the top. Broil the sandwiches until cheese gets melted for around 2 mins and starts to bubble, then serve the sandwiches hot.

48. Squash Fritters

(Ready in about 17 minutes | **Serving:** 4 | **Difficulty**:

Easy)

Per serving: **Kcal:** 200, **Fat:** 4 g, **Net Carbs**: 8 g,

Protein: 6 g

Ingredients:

- 3 oz. cream cheese

- 1 whisked egg

- ½ teaspoon dried oregano

- Salt

- Black pepper

- 1 yellow grated summer squash

- 1/3 cup grated carrot

- 2/3 cup breadcrumbs

- 2 tablespoons olive oil

Instructions:

1. Add all the ingredients to a bowl and toss to combine. Make patties out of the mixture and oil them. Place patties in the basket of fryer and toast for around 7 minutes.

49. Scallops and Dill

(Ready in about 15 minutes | **Serving:** 4 | **Difficulty**:

Easy)

Per serving: **Kcal:** 152, **Fat**: 4 g, **Net Carbs**: 19 g,

Protein: 4 g

Ingredients:

- 1 lb. debearded sea scallops

- 1 tablespoon lemon juice

- 1 teaspoon dill, chopped

- 2 teaspoons olive oil

- Salt

- Black pepper

Instructions:

1. Mix scallops with the rest of the ingredients in a bowl and shake to coat. Place in the basket of fryer and toast for around 5 minutes at 360°F. Enjoy with dill sauce on the side.

50. Italian Sandwich

(Ready in about 26 minutes | **Serving:** 2 | **Difficulty:** Easy)

Per serving: Kcal: 324, **Fat:** 16 g, **Net Carbs**: 39 g, **Protein**: 12 g

Ingredients:

*   1 sliced eggplant

- 2 teaspoons dried parsley

- Salt

- Black pepper

- ½ cup breadcrumbs

- ½ teaspoon Italian seasoning

- ½ teaspoon garlic powder

- ½ teaspoon onion powder

- 2 tablespoons milk

- 4 bread slices

- Cooking spray

- ½ cup mayonnaise

- ¾ cup tomato sauce

- 2 cups grated mozzarella cheese

Instructions:

1. Season eggplants with pepper and salt and place aside for 10 minutes. Mix breadcrumbs with parsley, Italian seasoning, garlic, onion, pepper, and salt. Mix mayo with milk in another bowl. Dip eggplant in mayo mixture and then in crumbs and place in the basket of the fryer. Toast for around 15 minutes at 400°F. Brush bread with oil and add parmesan and mozzarella on both bread slices. Add eggplant, basil, and tomato, and add bread on top.

Conclusion

Eating well and healthy is possible with the help of hot air fryers. They are also called oil-less fryers, but the correct term to define these excellent appliances is hot air fryer.

As you may have noticed when preparing these various recipes, it is a fryer that does not need oil to cook fried or other foods. The result is not quite the same as that of a traditional fryer, but quite similar. In addition, it has a great advantage: it fries not only food but also bakes, roasts or toasts it. All this is done by cooking the food with hot air circulating at high temperature and at a certain speed, simulating the way food is cooked with oil.

All you have to do is introduce the food, program the type and time of cooking and let the fryer do its job. In short, these fryers stand out for their ease of use and their thermal and electrical safety, in addition to giving you the possibility of preparing your favorite dishes or snacks without the hassle of fats.

CPSIA information can be obtained
at www.ICGtesting.com
Printed in the USA
BVHW092310270421
605945BV00010B/1123